# Peace of Mind

## By

## Tracy R. Offer

ISBN: 0-75964-105-6

This book is printed on acid free paper.

1stBooks – rev. 06/27/01

# Table of Contents

## Emotions From Within



## Puzzled Situations

# ***Just A Thought***

*Life is a funny thing.*
*We go through life day in and day out trying to make ends meet*
*We have all gone through many struggles in our lifetime (despite*
*our color)*

*We have our elders who have seen and gone through enough*
*They just sit and wait on the good Lord to return.*

*We all have elders who have taught or at least tried to*
*T each us knowledge and wisdom to survive the every day*
*struggles.*

*We have failed to listen to that knowledge and wisdom*
*Look at us now; look at our children*

*Remember long ago when everyone pitched in*
*With the upbringing of other children.*

*Now, our children are disrespectful;*
*Parents are afraid of their own children*

*Politicians are doing whatever they please*
*Races are fighting one another and the reasons*
*Aren't worth listening too.*

*Do you really think that God has the time to listen*
*To why you did what you did?*

*You will burn regardless of your explanations*
*He gave us a Bible full of commandments to follow*
*Do we?*

*Yes, it has been said the that Bible has been rewritten time and*
*time again*

*Oh, well the question still remains*
*Why aren't we doing what it says?*


*The Bible can be written over a thousand and one times*
*The fact still remains that there is a God*
*Either do good or do as you please.*


*We have lost our children, each other, and ourselves*
*What has happened to our world?*
*We are all fighting and no one is winning.*
*We all are suffering and will continue to suffer if we don't*
*change our ways*


*Yes, God loves us unconditionally*
*He was nailed to the cross for us*
*He saved us from sin*
*His blood cleansed our souls*


*And how do we thank him?*


*There are those that ask*
*Well, if he loves me why would he want me to burn in the lake of*
*fire?*
*Well, goodness if you love him, you wouldn't do wrong*
*He gives us a choice*
*We make mistakes; he pulls us out and once again*
*We make mistakes and he keeps pulling us out*


*You have cheated, robbed, stole, abused, fornicated, lied*
*Killed, and just lost your mind and you still question*
*As to why God would send you to Hell?*
*God said it and he did it*
*He never broke a promise*
*But look at all the promises we broke to him*
*Every time he pulled us out of something,*

*We prayed and swore never to do it again
Did you do it again or did you change?
Now a new year is near
Everyone is going crazy getting ready and preparing
For water shortage, electricity outage, computers
malfunctioning,
How much money is the ATM*

*Is anyone getting ready and preparing for the real **Y2K**
Yes 2 King Jesus*

*Tracy R. Offer
All rights reserved
Copyright: 12/99*

# <u>*Praise*</u>

*Lord, I praise thee*
*I sing, dance, and shout for glory*
*I do it all for you*

*You gave your life for me,*
*You endured pain and agony all for me*

*I dance with Glory on the Devil's head*
*Hey, hey Lord you are so good to me*

*I have been set free of all pain and iniquity*
*Now, I praise you with all my heart and soul*

*Praise the Lord; Praise the Lord*
*There's no other who can do what you do*
*Because of you I now sing, dance, walk, think, shout for joy*

*I love to Praise your name*

*Tracy R. Offer*
Copyright: 07/99

# ***<u>Believe It or Not</u>***

*We are all created different
Color, personality, character,
Priorities, knowledge, appearance*

*Some mature faster than others'
We all view life in a different way*

*No one is the same*

*It is up to the individual to live and learn
We can't pressure people into being what we
Think they should be or act the way we want them to act*

*We need to learn to live within ourselves
People can change; it takes time
God has something in store for us all,
So, who are we to say that nobody can change?*

*Are you God?*

*If we continue to live in the past,
The future will slip right by us
We are so full of negativity,
Just can't stand to see somebody give another person a chance*

*Chance and change is obviously something we fear*

*Like it or not believe it or not*
*People can, and do change*
*People deserve chances*

*God does it for you*

*Tracy R. Offer*
*Copyright: 07/99*
*All rights reserved*

# <u>Joy</u>

*My heart, soul so full of joy*
*The world so troubled, still I have joy*

*The pain, sorrow that try to keep me down*
*Still, I have joy*

*The name calling, the everyday struggles*
*Still, I have joy*

*You always know when the time is right*
*You bring many blessings my way*
*In turn, I am filled with more joy*

*There's nothing like feeling the joy*
*Of you flowing through my heart, mind, and soul*

*You bring great joy in my life*

*Lord, you are the true meaning of*

*Joy*

*Tracy R. Offer*
*Copyright: 07/99*

# ***<u>Time & Time Again</u>***

*Time and time again, you pray for the things you want*
*Not for what you need; you fail to realize why you aren't being*
*blessed*

*I am God, I know before you, I see before you*
*I know all*

*I know what you need, you see otherwise*
*I often give you signs letting you know what's right and what's*
*wrong*
*What should be and what shouldn't be*
*Still, you choose to do as you please*

*In due time you will get what you pray for but you must first trust*
*and believe*
*Second, you must realize what you "need"*

*I will not bless you with money and material things that are not*
*of me*
*I grant blessings when blessings are due*

*Blessings are not granted when you want them, but when I send*
*them*

*It's up to you to just live your life, let all other things be in my*
*hands*

*The more you interfere with problems, the more heartache*
*And pain will come your way just stand still and know that*
*I am God*

*These things you already know, you fail to abide by my rules*
*Look at where your way has gotten you*

*Time and Time Again*
*When will you learn, that my way is best*

*Tracy R. Offer*
*All Rights Reserved*
*Copyright: 12/99*

# ***<u>The Race</u>***

*Shopping sprees, sales of all kinds, you can't be late*

*Television interviews, new gossip, you just can't miss*

*Concerts of all kinds, new hairstyles, you can't be without*

*On a daily basis you race to everything*
*That will give you great pleasure and satisfaction*

*I am the one who can really give you what you need*

*Will you run that same race for me?*

*Tracy R. Offer*
*Copyright: 07/99*
*All rights reserved*

# <u>*I Gave You My Hand*</u>

*You were looking for a way out*
*You were sick with cancer*
*I gave you my hand*

*You lost a loved one*
*You were stressed and confused*
*I gave you my hand*

*You prayed and prayed to be free of all sickness and pain*
*I heard your cry, answered your prayers*
*Once again, I gave you my hand*

*The time has come*
*You stand proud, overwhelmed with excitement*
*You still stand, waiting to see my hand*

*Tracy R. Offer*
*Copyright: 07/99*
*All rights reserved*

# <u>*I Am He*</u>

*I am he who supplies your every need*
*I am he who gave you life*
*I am he who keeps you safe*
*I am he who feeds you when you have no food*
*I am he who makes a way to pay your bills when you have no*
*money*

*I am he who has power*
*The storms, the winds, the waters are fierce because of me*
*You stay safe, healthy because of me*
*Things are going so much better for you now all because of me*

*You have called my name "Jesus"*
*I made it better for you*
*Now, you call me no more*

*Just remember, I am he who*
*Has the key to the gates of Heaven*

*Tracy R. Offer*
*Copyright: 07/99*

# ***Remember When***

*Remember when grandma took you to church every Sunday?*

*Remember when you were taught what was of me and what was not?*

*Of course not, now you are so into fashion, money, power*
*Trying to see who you can out do*
*You have forgotten the values of life*
*Most of all you have forgotten me*

*Remember when you couldn't pay your bills*
*You were homeless*
*You had no idea where your next meal was coming from*
*When you were stranded with no one to call on but me*
*Your "best friend" let you down*

*Remember when you called my name "Jesus" every time you*
*were in need*
*Whenever you called I was there*
*Now you are doing so much better*
*You have stopped calling me*

*I see all, know all, hear all*
*When I return and open the gates of Heaven*
*Just Remember when*

*Tracy R. Offer*
*Copyright: 07/99*

*Tracy R. Offer*

# **<u>When</u>**

*When was the last time:*

*You helped someone elderly cross the street or carry their bags?*
*You told someone from the heart "I love you"?*
*You fed a hungry child?*
*Taught a child the difference between reality and fiction?*
*You had a family reunion?*
*You read the Bible?*
*Gave your tithes?*
*Went to church?*
*You sat down with a child and had a talk?*
*When was the last time you shared a special moment?*
*When was your last family gathering?*
*When was the last time you reached out to someone?*
*You gave a positive lecture?*
*You didn't judge someone?*
*You didn't mind other people's business?*

*When was the last time,*
*You asked God to come into your life?*

*Tracy R. Offer*
*Copyright: 07/99*

# ***Think First***

*Have you taken the time to think about*
*The life you have lived...*

*Every Sunday you are dressed in your best,*
*Your clothes cost too much to praise my name*

*The offering plate comes your way,*
*You put in a 1.00 the other 5.00 is for beer*

*Before entering my home you smoke/drink*
*Afterwards, the same thing*

*All this and you say you love me!*

*The doctor told you one thing; I did another*
*Your friends' betray you; I am still here,*
*You work hard and receive no rewards*
*Heaven has many rewards in store for you*

*After all I have done for you; still you don't know me*

*You choose to redeem your soul to the sinful lives of others'*

*It is I that keeps you, not your friends'*
*I am God, Alpha & Omega, The Beginning & The End*

*You dare forget me after dying on the cross for you*
*To save your dirty soul*

*It is you that needs me*
*Do you know of any that will give their life for you*
*Such as I have*

*Be careful of your decisions*
*Judgement Day is soon to come*

16

# ***The Front Line***

*The question is:*
*Do you love me?*
*The answer is:*
*Yes, Father I do?*

*You love me so that while on earth,*
*You never came to church to hear the word*
*Yet, you criticized others for not doing so*

*You watched the children play, tricked one and had your way*

*Your mother gave you life and love; she lays in the hospital bed*
*Wondering when you would be at her side*

*Your wife full of beauty, wisdom and strength, she stood at your*
*side no matter what*
*You were unable to deal with her strength, so you beat her down*

*You say you are doing my work*
*Well, my work never mentioned*
*Racism, terrorist attacks,*
*I never mentioned to do the Devil's work*

*You ask "If there's a God then why is my life so miserable?"*
*Well, now you stand here before me*
*Your life was full of misery because that's the route you chose*

*I left you a great book to abide by; you chose to follow your own*
*book*

*You think I don't exist because your prayers aren't answered on*
*time*
*You believe the world is here because of science*

*I am not science; I am God*
*The First, The Last*

*Now, that you are able to see I am real*
*What do you have to say about the life you have lived?*

*Being here at the front line*
*Can be good, it can be bad*
*It all depends on the life you had*

*Tracy R. Offer*

# <u>How Have You Lived Your Life</u>

*Hello, my child*
*What kind of lifestyle did you have?*

*Well Lord, I wasn't expecting you so soon*
*I don't think I was all that bad on earth*

*Mmm, what did I do?*
*I stole, robbed, cheated, molested, fornicated*
*Killed, tortured others*
*I basically did what I wanted*
*Who was gonna stop me, the law could never figure it out*
*Everyone was afraid to tell on me*

*So, my child you did all the things I asked you not to*
*Not once did you ever ask for forgiveness, I never saw your face*
*in church*
*You kept the Bible buried under books; you never said a prayer*

*Despite the lifestyle you lived, I kept you alive for many years*
*Not once did you show any appreciation for what I had done for*
*you*

*Now, you stand before me*
*Think of all you have done*
*Now, think of your after life*

*Tracy R. Offer*

*Copyright: 11/99*

# <u>*Heaven*</u>

*What a wonderful place to be*
*Peace, love, happiness*
*A place where we can all share a beautiful home with God.*

*Hell- a place we all hate*
*Yet, we do so much that will get us there first class*

*You praise God as much as you can*
*Just yesterday, you molested your child*

*You spread the gospel on a daily basis*
*Last week you were out stealing*

*You encourage others that God is the way*
*Last night you committed adultery*

*You talk about family values*
*You don't even acknowledge your own*

*You love to spend hundreds of dollars on fancy things*
*You can't even give God 10%*

*How can you want to be in Heaven*
*When you are doing things that*
*Will send you to Hell*

# ***How Deep is Your Hate***

*Despite being created by the same God*
*And being the same internally, you hate the opposite race*

*Your life is in danger*
*The only person that can save you is the "color" you hate*
*Will you choose to live or die?*

*A child is in need of help*
*You are the only one that can help but the "color" isn't right*
*Will you help or ignore the child?*

*You were raised by one of your parents,*
*You are taught to hate anyone that's not like you*
*Later you find that your absent parent*
*Is the "color" you have been taught to hate*
*Will you learn to love or continue to hate?*

*It is now Judgement Day*
*God is the "color" you have always hated*
*What do you do now?*

*Tracy R. Offer*
*Copyright: 08/99*

# <u>*Just The Opposite*</u>

*These are my commandments:*

1. *Thou shalt love the Lord thy God with all thy heart,*
   *With all thy soul with all thy mind*
2. *Thou shalt love thy neighbour*
3. *Thou shalt have no other Gods before me*
4. *Thou shalt not make any graven image or any likeness of*
   *anything That is in Heaven above, or that is in the earth*
   *beneath or that is the Water under the earth*
5. *Thou shalt not bow down thyself to them, nor serve them for*
   *I the Lord thy God am jealous*
6. *Thou shalt not take thy name of the Lord thy God in vain*
7. *Remember the Sabbath Day to keep it holy*
8. *Honour thy father and thy mother that thy day may be long*
   *upon the Land which the Lord thy God giveth thee*
9. *Thou shalt not kill*
10. *Thou shalt not commit adultery*
11. *Thou shalt not steal*
12. *Thou shalt not bear false witness against thy neighbour*
13. *Thou shalt not covet thy neighbours house, wife, nor his*
    *Manservant, nor his maidservant, nor his ox, nor his ass, nor*
    *Anything that is thy neighbours*

*You do just the opposite*
*Yet, you still wish to be welcomed into Heaven*

# <u>*In Reference To Your Letter*</u>

*I received your letter the other day*
*I have to say all the things you say and do are true*

*But listen at what I have in store for you*

*When I sat down for dinner last night*
*I blessed my food and so did my children*

*When I lay down to sleep*
*I thanked the Lord for another safe day*
*So did my children*

*When I rose, I thanked the Lord for seeing another day*
*My children did too.*

*It's your fault you are no longer in Heaven not anyone else's*
*You are at fault for trying to be greedy*

*There are those who enjoy living the life you provide*
*As for myself, I got sick of it*

*I get tempted just like anyone else*
*To distract myself from doing wrong*
*I hum heavenly hymns*

*I teach my children about God*
*Your way of living is nothing but trouble*

*You have put many obstacles in my way*
*And no matter how difficult you made it, God moved it out of my*
*way*

*Tracy R. Offer*

*See, through God all things are possible*
*And because in my heart and mind that's what I believe,*
*There's nothing you can do to bring me down*

*As for sharing a home with you*
*Ha, I don't think so.*

*I refuse to let you have me twice*

*Tracy R. Offer*
*All rights reserved*
*Copyright: 11/99*

# ***The Time Is Now***

You have worked hard all week long
*You have partied all weekend
Sunday you stayed in bed all day*

*You just got a raise; you still walk by those in need
You don't even give me my share*

*Your enemies continue to harm you; finally you want revenge*

*The thunders roar, the skies lights fiercely
Is it time?*

*The rain pours harshly; the storms are heavy
Is it time?*

*The clouds darken; the sky begins to open
Is it time?*

*Have you made up your mind?
For we know not when it is time
We often try so hard to live right, yet we still manage to stray
Time is running out, there's no turning back*

*It is time to make that change*

*Tracy R. Offer
Copyright: 07/99
All rights reserved*

# ***This Is My Prayer***

*Hello Father,*
*It is me again, here to make my last and final cry*
*I am tired, and weak*
*The trials and tribulations you send my way*
*Are to make me strong, but I can no longer handle them*

*Lord, I am here on my bending knees to confess*
*And ask for forgiveness for all my wrong doings*

*Please take away all of me that is not of you*
*I am ready to walk like you, talk like you, love like you*
*Forgive like you, I am ready to walk with you*

*After all my sins you still stand by my side*
*In sickness, health, stress, happiness, sorrow*
*You have been a better friend to me than I have been to myself*
*Lord, I am ready to live like you*

*Tracy R. Offer*
*Copyright: 07/99*
*All rights reserved*

# *<u>My Life</u>*

*Is it really my life?*

*Everyone is so into my life*
*Judging me, degrading me*
*Advising me, gossiping about me*

*What about your life?*
*What are you doing with yourself?*
*How dare you be so judgmental of me*

*There's nothing wrong with being helpful, but let's not get*
*carried away*

*Everyone needs someone to talk to*
*Or we will go crazy keeping things bottled inside*
*But, that doesn't give you the right to get too involved in my life*

*We all need someone to share things with, whether it's good or*
*bad*
*You may give your opinion, or you may say nothing*
*But please don't live my life*

*You are no better than me; you have problems too*
*What are you doing with yourself?*

*Life is difficult for us all, but we can't live another person's life*
*We can only support them in their time of need*
*Learn to take care of our own lives*

*My life is my life*
*Your life Is your life*

28

*Tracy R. Offer*
*Copyright: 07/99*

# *<u>Why Walk Alone</u>*

*There have been many times, when you have cried to me*

*You poured your heart out when you were down*

*I could tell you meant every word from the heart,*
*Then when I made things better, you forget me*

*I tell you time and time again, let not your heart be troubled*
*Still you try and solve things on your own*

*I promised you, I would never leave nor forsake you*
*Still you rely on "friends" for help*

*I asked you to*
*Lay your burden upon me for I will give you rest*
*Still you choose to handle your troubles and take on other's*

*I will only give you what you can handle*
*Still you choose to take more than you can handle*

*You fail to realize that I am God*
*You fail to realize what I can do*

*I ask you to stand still and know that I am God*
*You choose to chase everything*

*Only I can fight a battle and win*
*You choose to fight and loose.*

*I am God*
*All things are possible through me*
*I am everything you need and more*

*When you are sad I can make you happy*
*And you won't even have to regret it.*

*Your lifestyle isn't what you want*
*You made it that way yourself, with faith the size of a mustard*
*seed*
*You can change all that makes you miserable*

*Yet, you still cry at night asking*
*Why are you walking alone?*

# ***<u>Reminisce And Realize</u>***

*There was a time when*
*Your life was filled with many trials and tribulations*
*No matter how hard you tried, nothing ever went right for you*
*Finally, one day you did something that should have done long*
*ago.*

*You got down on your knees and cried out with all your might*
*Still, things weren't better right away*
*Still, you continued to cry out for help*
*I answered only the prayers that you needed*
*The prayers you wanted are the same ones that kept you in*
*despair*

*Your lifestyle has changed for the better*
*You pray, you pay your tithes, you are employed*
*You have your own home; you have a great family*

*The happiness of your lifestyle has put a permanent glow on*
*your face*

*You meet an old friend*
*Slowly, but surely you begin to backslide*

*You are back out at the clubs; you are seeing other women*
*You ignore your children; you are behind in your tithes*
*You are completely lost AGAIN*

*The same way I pulled you out of despair*
*I can let go and you'll be back to the way you were*

*There's a reason I answer prayers*
*There's a reason I turn lives around*
*There's a reason I pull you out of darkness*

*I love you*

*Nothing good will come to you with this lifestyle*
*Remember the way you were before me*
*Remember the way you were when you met me*
*Look at you now that you are drifting away from me*

*Tracy R. Offer*
*All Rights Reserved*
*Copyright: 01/00*

# How Dare You

*If there were no me, there would be no you*
*How dare you say you don't believe*

*You awaken every day by me*
*You have breath by me*
*You can see, hear, walk, laugh, all because of me*
*How dare you call it luck*

*The trees, the animals, the waters, the world*
*I created so beautifully, has been destroyed*
*How dare you question why things don't go right for you*

*The people, I created all colors, all personalities*
*How dare you make mockery of them*

*You make millions; I only ask 10%*
*How dare you question why you have no money*

*You are a star; I gave you many talents*
*You refuse to look inside and see what you're really worth*
*How dare you question why you have nothing*

*I made you what you are; yet you go and redo my work*
*How dare you question why you don't look right*

*You can enjoy all the riches in Heaven with me*
*Yet you chose to enjoy the riches of Hell*
*How dare you call my name only in the time of need*

*I made the world; I can take the world*
*You have destroyed my creation; you have destroyed each other*
*You abuse my children*
*You disrespect your elders those who made things easier for*
*your future*
*When I return and you do not hear your name called to come*
*home*
*How dare you question why you weren't chosen*

*Tracy R. Offer*
*Copyright: 07/99*
*All rights reserved*

# <u>*My Friend*</u>

*When I needed an ear*
*You were there to listen*

*When I needed a shoulder*
*You gave me yours*

*When I was broke*
*You gave me your last*

*When I was lonely*
*You kept me company*

*When I was hurt*
*You shared my pain*

*When I am happy*
*You share my joy*

*When I succeed*
*You congratulate me*

*When I just want to be me*
*You are still there for me*

*Thank you for being*
*My friend*

*Dedicated to:*
*Tisha Natria Johnson*

*Tracy R. Offer*
*Copyright: 07/99*

*Tracy R. Offer*

# <u>***Children***</u>

*Center of all our hearts*

*Happiness that fulfills our lives*

*Images of the future*

*Love that over whelms our sadness*

*Dreams we all wish for*

*Remembrance of our own childhood*

*Emotions with no prejudice*

*Noble spirits*

*To think of all the things we can learn from them*
*Look at what we teach them*

*Tracy R. Offer*
*Copyright: 07/99*
*All rights reserved*

# <u>*Children Are Our Future*</u>

*We say children are our future:*
*We limit their education; we don't respect them*
*We beat their brains out; leave them homeless*

*We say children are our future:*
*We refuse to feed them; we don't teach them right from wrong*
*We can't control them; we allow them to control each other*
*And we continue to bury them over senseless crimes*

*We say children are our future:*
*We spend more time on plotting what country to destroy*
*Instead of what countries to save*
*Yet, we only have time and money to live glamorous lives*

*How will children be our future if we continue to destroy them?*

*Tracy R. Offer*
*Copyright: 07/99*
*All rights reserved*

*Tracy R. Offer*

# <u>*My Babies*</u>

*I brought you in this world, not knowing what to do,*
*Not knowing how I would take care of you*

*As you began to grow, many things about you began to change*
*Your fingers, toes, eyes, hair, nose*

*You began to crawl; then you started walking*
*What was I to do?*
*Still not knowing what was in store for us*
*Times began to get difficult, things got confusing*
*It was all very new and challenging for me*

*I began to pray*
*Lord, for I know not what I am doing*
*You have blessed me with double joy*
*Still what am I to do?*
*Which way am I to go?*
*This is such a challenge; I need your guidance*
*I need strength, patience, and courage*
*I ask to be blessed with all the knowledge*
*All the love it takes to be a parent*

*I pray that I am able to teach my babies to trust and believe only*
*in you*
*To stay together, and let no one destroy the bond they have*
*developed*

*My babies*
*You are as one*

*Dedicated to:*
*Naa'irah Sade Parker*
*Eliyah Iman Parker*

*Tracy R. Offer*
*Copyright: 07/99*

# ***<u>One Love</u>***

*God has blessed me with two beautiful children*
*Throughout your lifetime people will try to hurt you*

*You are two people that share the same love*
*A love that no man/woman can destroy*

*A love that will make you stronger*
*No matter what trials may come your way*

*A love that will keep you together*
*No matter how far apart you may be*

*Your love will allow you to be at each other's side*
*For support, strength, wisdom and guidance*

*Neither man, nor woman will have*
*The strength to destroy something so special*

*You have been blessed with God's love and my love*
*A love that's too powerful to be destroyed; yet too strong to be*
*misunderstood*

*You are as one, no matter what life brings your way or what*
*others may do*

*You are to stand strong*
*And know that God will handle all of your problems*

*A love that will last forever*

*Dedicated to:*
*Naa'irah S. Parker*
*Eliyah I. Parker*

*Tracy R. Offer*
*Copyright: 12/99*
*All rights reserved*

# <u>*Sisterhood*</u>

*You have become beautiful young women*
*You have developed a strong relationship*

*There will be times in life when*
*You don't get along or may not agree on everything*

*There will be times when others will become jealous*
*Of your achievements, or just be jealous of you*

*Life is a funny thing, there's so much to learn*
*So much to see there's just so much of everything*

*No matter what happens in your life*
*You are not to let anyone cause you to depart*

*Jealousy, smiling faces, men, life itself*
*If you are unable to handle*
*The trials and tribulations that come your way*
*Please pray, don't turn against one another*
*You are as one, trust God, trust each other*
*Love each other; be there for each other*
*Please, Please*
*Let no one destroy what the two of you have*

*Dedicated to:*
*Naa'irah Sade Parker*
*Eliyah Iman Parker*

*Tracy R. Offer*
*Copyright: 07/99*

# *<u>The Struggles You May Encounter</u>*

*I brought you into a world that was once friendly*

*Life now, can be very challenging*
*You must control your life; let not life control you*

*Don't be fooled by those smiling faces, for they will sometimes*
*be your worse enemy*

*Don't be fooled by your "friends'" they too know not the*
*meaning of friendship*

*Friendship can be a very meaningful relationship, if there is*
*trust and love*

*Trust is very important, though you can't trust many*

*To survive in this world, you must believe and trust in God*
*Have trust for one another; be strong for yourself as well as*
*each other*
*Love yourself; believe in yourself*

*The struggles you may encounter will not prevail*
*If you just believe*

*Dedicated to:  Naa'irah Parker*
*Eliyah Parker*
*Zakia Ritchie*
*Malik Ritchie*

*Tracy R. Offer*
*Copyright: 08/99*

# <u>***My Prayer To You***</u>

*Drugs- destruction for life*
*Money- earn honestly*
*Friends- be ware of smiling faces*
*Rumors -you know in your heart what's true*
*Relationships- be careful, be wise*
*Violence- be strong, don't let it happen*


*Lord,*
*I pray that these precious children*
*Are taught or at least have an idea*
*Of what it means to take heed to your every command*

*Please, guide them towards a positive path in life*
*Let them not stray away from you*
*Bless them with courage, wisdom, love*
*When times are hard, and challenging; when they have no one at*
*their side*
*I want them to know they can call on you*
*You can be more to them than they can be to themselves*
*I pray they learn the best way to survive is through you*


*Dedicated to:*
*Naa' irah Sade Parker*
*Eliyah Iman Parker*
*Malik Ritchie*
*Zakia Ritchie*

*Tracy R. Offer*
*Copyright: 07/99*
*All rights reserved*

# <u>*Do You Have Any Idea*</u>

*You are young, beautiful*
*And full of many unknown talents*

*You are so full of life and laughter*
*Let no one take away what you are*

*Beauty is outside and within*
*It belongs to you despite what anyone else says*

*You have much to accomplish*
*Just look within and be strong*

*All the negativity that surrounds you*
*Needs to be left alone*

*You know what's right and what's wrong*
*You must realize that being you is something no one else can be*

*Once you are gone, whose gonna do the things you do*
*No one else can take care of mamma like you*
*No one can smile like you; no one can brighten a room as you do*

*A man that can watch the pain of his love, is no man*

*A man that "loves" will be there for his love no matter what*

*You can be so much more with or without him*
*While you are 6 feet under,*
*He will still be here breathing the air you should*
*He will still be here with his family and friends'*
*While your family and friends will mourn you 24/7*

*There are so many things people say about love*
*Love is blind, love hurts, love feels good*
*But they failed to mention that*
*Love can be the death of you*

*Please, look within and see that you*
*Are an important tool in God's plan.*

*Tracy R. Offer*
*All rights reserved*
*Copyright: 12/99*

# <u>*My Dear Sweet Child*</u>

*For many years you have struggled*
*With all types of trials & tribulations*

*I have been there for you every time*
*Still, you fail to acknowledge me*

*You are so unhappy and full of misery*
*I called your name; you fail to hear*

*Look around you,*
*How do you think you have made it this far?*

*I am what you need*
*Friends and men are only out to get you*

*You can't find a friend truer than me;*
*I will never leave nor forsake you*
*I can put your heart and mind at ease*

*My dear sweet child, I have died on the cross for you*
*I am calling your name*
*I am at your side every moment of the day*
*Why have you failed to respond?*

*You must have it in your heart to trust and believe*
*You must be willing to give up the men*
*Your so-called friends, drugs*

*I told you, if you take one step I'll take two*
*There's so much in store for you happiness*
*Success, love, comfort*
*All you have to do, is make the first move*

*My dear sweet child accept me in your life*
*As I have accepted you in mine*

*Who will it be me or them?*

*Tracy R. Offer*

*Copyright: 12/99*

# <u>*Patience, My Child*</u>

*You may feel as though
I don't see your struggle*

*You may feel as though
I don't hear your cry*

*My child
Every pain you feel I feel
Every tear you cry I cry*

*In your prayers you ask for things you already have
You fail to look deep within and explore yourself*

*You were just a stem
Now, you have blossomed into a beautiful rose*

*Look closely and feel your spirit
Young, beautiful, strong, wise
Full of knowledge and courage*

*It takes time to discover many things about yourself
Patience will bring you many things
Rushing will cause many things to pass you by*

*My dear child just being you is a talent,
No one else can do the things I have in store for you*

*My sweet child, you have more than you know*
*It will all come to light in due time*

*Patience, My child*

*Dedicated to:*
*Angie Thomas*

*Tracy R. Offer*

# ***Once Upon a Childhood***

*Young, pretty born into a world*
*Loved by many family and friends*

*Time goes on*
*Now, a bit older*
*Able to know what's going on but not understanding*

*Good times, bad times, horrible times*
*Laughter, mistakes, torture*

*No mother, no father, just God and me*

*All grown up now, still facing the same problems*
*Life is fill of trials and tribulations, but I have made it through*

*If only you could have been there*
*For love, support, protection*

*We both missed a lot from each other*

*If you could see me now*
*Stronger, wiser, mature, successful, just all grown up*

*As long as we both remain on this earth, it's not too late for us to*
*reunite*

*We can share so much, do so many things*
*Please don't let time take us further apart*

*Tracy R. Offer*

> *At night I lay dreaming of finding you*
> *I pray we share the same dream*
>
> *I Love You*

*Tracy R. Offer*
*Copyright: 08/99*
*All rights reserved*

# <u>*A Mother's Prayer*</u>

*If I should die this very day, please don't cry for me*
*I am in a better place; there's no pain and suffering here*

*I ask that you stay strong, continue praying*
*My lost is painful to many,*
*I truly understand what you are going through*

*Mom will always be in your heart*
*We have shared great times together,*
*Our memories will keep you in spirit*

*My greatest wish is that you keep a clear, positive mind*
*Let no one turn you into something you're not,*
*Hold on to God's unchanging hand trust and believe*

*You must know with all your might*
*That God will never leave nor forsake you*
*He will be everything you need and more*

*I am with you always*
*I will be at your side in good and bad times*

*Some will try to guide you in the path of darkness*
*I will be there to show you the light*

*You will live in a world of dishonesty*
*I will be there to show you the truth*

*Some will try to rob you of your pride, dignity*
*Strength and courage*

*You are still a part of me*
*They will fail at everything*

*Tracy R. Offer*

*Judgement Day is soon to come*
*There I will stand waiting to take your hand*

*Mommy loves you dearly*

*Dedicated to:*
*Naa'irah S. Parker*
*Eliyah I. Parker*

*Tracy R. Offer*
*All rights reserved*
*Copyright: 09/99*

# <u>*A Child's Prayer*</u>

*My days on earth were filled with great pleasure,*
*I enjoyed all the birthday parties, sleepovers,*
*Shopping sprees, most of all your love for me.*

*Please, don't hold a grudge*
*Do not feel you have lost everything*

*I felt no pain*
*I have much to gain being here with God*

*Angels will watch you day and night*
*I will still be at your side every second*

*Mamma,*
*I will never let go of our loving memories,*
*We shared so much together*
*I want you to be strong, keep your head up*
*There's nothing you can do to fix the pain*
*And suffering you go through*
*God will take care of everything*

*I want you to keep praying, don't cry for me*
*Be happy that I am in a place*
*Where nothing but good will come to me*
*Soon, you will be able to live a peaceful life with me*

*I know it's hard to loose your most precious gift*
*Every night, I hear your cry*

*I have good news*
*When you weep, I wipe away your tears*
*When you smile for no reason, it's me singing in your heart*
*When you are cold, it's me that light's the fireplace to keep you*
*warm*

*They have taken away my body*
*But my soul will be with you for all eternity*

*I am with you always*

# ***Thank You***

*I would like to take this time to thank you for so many things*

*When I came into this world with no where to go, you were there*

*As life went on, I had many trials and tribulations*
*Wanting so much to give up*

*You showed me another way*

*You gave me your wisdom, your strength, your courage*
*Most importantly, you gave me your love and support*

*If God had not blessed me with a grandma like you,*
*I wonder where would I be?*

*Because of you I have become*
*A stronger, wiser person*

*While others are trying to bring me down*
*I am still able to stand strong and proud*

*You gave me your all*
*Now, I shall pass the same on to my children*

*I have been blessed a thousand times*
*Having you as my grandma*
*I have been blessed a million times*

*Thank you- Great Grandma*

*Dedicated To:*
*Elizabeth Ann Smith/Pinkney/Long*

*Tracy R. Offer*

*Copyright:09/99*

*Tracy R. Offer*

# ***<u>Second Time Around</u>***

*In the beginning things were grand*
*We went places, shared dreams and thoughts*

*Smiling times seemed as if they would last forever*

*Suddenly, things began to change for the worst*
*What went wrong?*
*Who is at fault?*

*How could something so good, so strong go so badly?*

*All my love, heart, soul, my everything*
*I gave it all*

*Did I give too much of myself?*
*Did I love you too much?*

*Now, we both look forward to being together again*
*How would it be the second time around?*
*Will we trust again, love again, share dreams and thoughts*
*again*
*Can we talk, not argue and fight?*
*Can we make love, not just do it?*
*Can we have walks in the park by the lake?*
*Can we sit and watch the clouds sail across the blue skies?*

*Have we learned from our past mistake*
*To make the second time around better*

*The second time around will it be stronger than the first*

*Tracy R. Offer*
*Copyright: 07/99*

# ***You Were My All***

*What a time we had*
*Going places, sharing things*
*Buying gifts, holding one another*
*Taking walks under the stars*

*Oh, we had a ball*
*Our relationship began to change*

*You were out all night*
*Barely worked during the day*

*You would boast that you were doing so much*
*When really you were doing so little*

*You left me in the cold*
*Still, I showed you love*

*You forgot all about me, until you needed something*

*As times began to change for the better for me*
*And worsen for you, then you were ready to commit.*

*You began to realize that it was me that made you what you are*

*It was me at your side, not your friends*
*Whenever you were in trouble, it was me who helped you.*

*Now, you fail to understand why my feelings aren't the same*
*How can you not know?*

*Tracy R. Offer*

*Why can't you move on?*
*Are you afraid of being alone?*
*Do you fear that no one else will want you?*
*Are you having thoughts that what you did to others will be done*
*to you?*

*Where is your independence, your strength?*
*Where is your dignity?*

*Because you were so selfish, self centered, obnoxious, and a fool*

*You lost all of me*
*You were my all*

# ***You Are Truly Special***

*In the beginning, I thought you were like the others*
*As time went on you showed me another side of what being a*
*"man" is*

*Your laughter, your conversations, your touch is something I*
*dream of having 24/7*
*Making passionate love with you- I long for every second*

*Someone like you deserves the very best in life*
*Never settle for second best*

*Your personality has helped me to be strong again*
*Your touch has helped me to feel comfort*
*Your smile lets me know you are trustworthy*

*You as a person; has really helped to make a difference in my*
*life*

*I wish you happiness and success in all that you do*
*If no one ever told you*

*You Are Truly Special*

*Tracy R. Offer*

*Copyright:09/99*

# <u>***Because Of You***</u>

*I was so unhappy, thinking my world had fallen apart*
*Wondering what could possibly make it better*

*To meet someone else was the furthest thing from my mind,*
*To go through all the ups and downs of love*
*I could never handle more than once*

*I met you, despite how I was feeling*
*You made me laugh, all the down-falls of a relationship*
*Began to look brighter because of you*

*Without even trying, you did so much to keep me happy*
*I now long to feel your touch, see your smile*
*Hear your voice; be at your side*

*Having a relationship...*
*Just to be with you, would be the best gift of all*
*Because of you, I now look forward to loving again*

*Tracy R. Offer*
*Copyright: 07/99*

# ***The Way You Make Me Feel***

*You send chills through my body without being in your presence*

*Your kindness, patience, sense of humor, understanding, most of
all
Your strong, warm embrace brings comfort
To my world letting me know that I am not alone*

*As the sun-sets, and the moon rises
I lay gazing at the stars holding myself
Wishing it were you at my bedside
To feel your masculine body pressed against mine*

*If I had one wish, it would be to be yours forever
You are a dear friend, great lover,
No matter what, I will always do my best to be there for you
I hope and pray that our friendship will never end*

*Finally, I have found
A man of character, a man of his word
A man that makes me feel safe, secure
A man that knows how to make a woman feel*

*I love The Way You Make Me Feel*

*Tracy R. Offer
Copyright: 03/99
All rights reserved*

# <u>*A Wish*</u>

*For so long I have carried the load of love*
*Happiness, sadness, stress, pleasure, pain*

*As time passed, so did my love*
*I told myself never again will I love*

*Here, I sit watching the clouds sail across the dark blue sky*
*Wishing love never existed because of all its changes*

*Suddenly, I meet someone that I can love more than my first love*
*Wishing I could tell him, show him my all*
*I wish I could share every moment and every emotion with him*
*His pain, happiness, sorrows, his all*

*A pleasurable wish of our making passionate love from dusk*
*until dawn*
*Feeling the heat of passion seeping through his soft skin,*
*Feeling the sweat pour from his masculine body onto mine*

*For him to feel the same is simply just*
*A WISH*

# ***Cherishing the Moment***

*I still remember meeting you for the first time*
*I still remember the first time we made love*

*After all this time, I still have you on my mind*

*You are so unique in more ways than one*
*Your touch has left a memory for a lifetime*

*All I think of is having you one more time*
*How can such a moment last so long?*

*You are what I have been searching for*
*For so long, still I can't have you*

*It feels as though we were meant to be*
*But can't be*

*You mean so much to me without even knowing*
*Being with you really made me feel special*

*I find myself in a daze thinking of only you*
*Oh, how I wish it could be true*

*Your touch*
*Your strength*
*Your love is all so gentle*

*I wish I could have more than just*
*Cherishing the Moment*

# <u>*If*</u>

*If I could have you for me*
*I would be very happy*

*What went wrong?*
*Things seemed to be going so well*

*I call, you're never home*
*I leave messages, you don't respond*

*Being with you was so grand*
*I am trying to understand*

*If I could hear your soothing voice again*
*Be with you just one more time*

*If we could plan a special evening*
*I am sure the memories would last a lifetime*

*A night of conversation, laughter*
*Caressing, having red wine under the stars*
*Holding one another, making passionate love for the last time*

*If I could just have you one more time*

*Tracy R. Offer*
*Copyright: 07/99*

# <u>*Be Mine*</u>

*Have you any idea how much
I dream of having you*

*Seeing you in my mind
Tossing, turning, sweat pouring*

*Your strong touch, your soft skin,
Your voice so deep; yet so smooth*

*Your presence so relaxing
Your embrace so comforting*

*Ugh, what I wouldn't do to have you
What will it take for you to be mine?*

*Tracy R. Offer
Copyright: 07/99*

# ___Missing You___

*Sleepless nights, no more warm embraces*
*No more laughter, no more passionate nights together*
*No more walks under the stars*

*All of you and everything about you*
*I am missing*

*What will bring back those hand-hand walks?*
*The laughter, the embraces, the passionate nights*
*What will bring you back?*

*I need to feel your special touch*
*Hear your soothing voice*

*I never thought such things could happen to me*
*I never imagined a man having that something about him*
*That would overwhelm my body, heart, soul, and mind*

*You are gone; I may never see you again*
*One day this letter may reach you*
*If so, you will know that I am*

*Missing you*

*Tracy R. Offer*
*Copyright: 07/99*

# *Is It You*

*One day a friend asked*

*"What type of man are you looking for?"*

*After a few minutes of carefully thinking,*
*I replied*

*"I am looking for a man who will":*
*Love me for me*
*Share thoughts and dreams together*
*Lotion my back after a shower*
*Have picnics and walks in the park*
*Support me no matter what*
*Send a card or rose just because*
*Listen to my sorrows and joys*
*Strong (mentally/physically), wise, trustworthy*
*Join me on a spiritual journey*
*Take my hand in marriage and cherish our love forever*

*Is this man you?*

*Tracy R. Offer*
*All rights reserved*
*Copyright: 12/99*

*Tracy R. Offer*

# ***<u>Once Upon A Dream</u>***

*There was a time when I dreamed of loving the perfect man*

*My relationships weren't as meaningful as I had hoped*

*Time and time again*
*I was being hurt, then happy, then hurt again*
*I cried and I cried*

*All the heartaches and pains made me a stronger person*

*I promised myself never will I love again*
*I told myself I'd rather be alone*

*Surprisingly, I met a handsome man*
*Who also had a few bad relationships*

*We talked, we laughed*
*We exchanged experiences*

*Finally, we exchanged emotions*

*It was all so grand; it was something I had never before*
*experienced*

*His skin like chocolate, his embrace so mighty, yet comforting*
*His love so heavenly*

*My dream lover has finally come to me*
*So I thought*

*I did everything possible to continue this dream into reality*

*Things have changed, but my feelings and dreams are
everlasting*

*It was short but oh so sweet
Thank you for your sweet intimacy*

*Tracy R. Offer
All rights reserved
Copyright: 12/99*

*Tracy R. Offer*

# ***<u>Confusion</u>***

*Why is it so easy to purchase the latest vehicle*
*Yet, so difficult to feed a hungry child*

*We teach our children to tell the proper authorities*
*About child abuse/ drug abuse, then we scold them for doing so*

*We teach and preach about stopping the violence*
*Yet, we allow our children to play the violent games*
*Watch the violent shows, and hear the violent songs*

*You are unable to have kids',*
*Then when you are finally blessed with a child*
*You choose to end his/her life*

*We love our mothers'/fathers' dearly,*
*They have given us so much love and taught us*
*So much about life, but we put them in homes and never visit*

*We give to charities from the heart*
*Then want the money back at the end of the year*

*You say you are my friend*
*When I called on you, where were you?*

*You say you love me*
*But you were just with someone else*

*For the New Year let's try to walk what we talk*
*And stop misleading our children as well as ourselves*
*The younger generation are the future,*
*We must get it together for us all to have better lives*


*Confusion will only lead to more destruction*


*Tracy R. Offer*
*Copyright: 12/99*
*All Rights Reserved*

*Tracy R. Offer*

# ***Is It Okay***

*Our children are living in a fantasy world of*
*Fashion, money, and power*

*Is it okay to allow our children to view life in such a*
*Manner without any explanation to follow*

*Models:*
*Are portrayed as the most beautiful people*
*In the world, our children put themselves through Hell*
*To look just like them*

*Magazines:*
*Tell our children in order to look good*
*They need to have a cigarette in one hand, and a 40 oz..*
*In the other*

*Videos:*
*Tell our children, that being sexy*
*Is wearing tight clothes or no clothes at all*

*Talk Shows:*
*Portray the lives of others as a good life*
*Sleeping with lots of men/women and in reply*
*You get an outstanding applause*

*As parents and as advertisers*
*We need to find a better way*
*To encourage our children that they are fine just as they are*

*No matter what size, big or small*
*No model can be as special as they are*

*Being healthy is loving themselves, not destroying themselves*
*with drugs*

*Being sexy is being smart and strong*

*A real man/woman will love you for you, not because of what
you wear*

*Is it okay to think our children's ideas are harmless?*

*Is it okay to let our children express themselves freely?
When there could be a possibility that they are
Loosing sight of what life is really about*

*As a nation, is it okay to just let things be?*

*Tracy R. Offer
All Rights Reserved
Copyright: 01/00*

*Tracy R. Offer*

# ***The Lost of Innocence***

*I am awakened by the sweet sound of birds chirping*
*The sun shines bright, the grass smells fresh*

*Here I play at the park*
*Swinging, climbing, running*

*As the day-light gets dim*
*I lay resting in the fresh green grass, watching the sun-set*

*Suddenly, something feels strange*
*I no longer feel peace of mind*

*A strong hand grabs me*
*I am unable to see the face*
*I can only see the sky spinning*

*This hand isn't friendly; it's so powerful*
*My voice is too soft for anyone to hear,*
*My body young and weak*

*All sorts of things are happening*
*I am so full of fear, pain, and anxiety*

*Most of all I am full of confusion*
*What have I done wrong?*
*I am only a child, what am I to do*
*To make this pain and fear go away*

*I am here in this world because God brought me here*
*Who are you to steal my pride and joy?*
*You touch me in places I never even knew existed*
*Who are you to take away my innocence?*

*I am a child of God*
*I am here to enjoy life, enjoy my family and friends'*
*I have done you no harm*
*So, why are you harming me?*

*What gives you the right to take away from others'?*
*You may think you are somebody now*
*On Judgement Day who will you be?*

*The Lost of Innocence has caused*
*Many trials and tribulations in my life*
*But it has also made me stronger with God's help.*

*Tracy R. Offer*

*Copyright: 10/99*

Tracy R. Offer

# *I Am Only Three*

I am only three with so much of the world to see
I live here in this place and it's all such a disgrace

My mamma drinks, sleeps, gets high
She even sells her body with me at her side

Over and over again strange people have come
To help us but her mind still flees

I am three and possibly sick with a disease
I don't go to the doctor's I just lay here and sleep

I am unable to interact with other kids'
I don't even get out to enjoy God's fresh air

I am only able to see and smell the filth that surrounds me
Where are those people to set me free?

I stand in the window crying for help
But no one understands me; I am only three

Mamma, why are you doing this to me
You are suppose to love me, not destroy me

I am one of God's most precious creations
Yet, you choose to only fulfill your sensations

What about me?
How could you possibly value Satan's work more than God's?

Still, I stand here waiting by the window crying with all my heart

*Why doesn't any one hear me?*

*Lord, please help me to be free of all this iniquity*
*I am young, lost and confused*
*I know my life isn't suppose to be this way*
*But my family has gone astray*
*Lord, as I continue to grow please*
*Bless me with strength, wisdom, and knowledge*
*I want to be better than my family*

*Lord, please send someone to help me*
*I am only three*

*Tracy R. Offer*
*Copyright:12/99*
*All Rights reserved*

# ***<u>Triflin</u>***

*You sit in the house 24/7*
*You get high, drink, and beg*

*How many more times will you be seen*
*Having oral sex with your child at your side?*

*How many more times will your "friends"*
*Talk about you, then be in your face?*

*How many more times will you degrade yourself for 5.00?*
*How often are you gonna let these "men" treat you like shit?*

*They don't care about you*
*The word is out honey, that you ain't nothing but a half cent*
*trollop*

*You sit around talking about how you gonna change*
*You are so tired of living your life this way*

*You know that's all a crop of crap, you don't care about yourself*
*That's why no one else does*

*If you were really tired, you would get a job*
*You wouldn't be caught in the bushes*
*Your child would know the real meaning of love*

*You are just another hopeless statistic, and that is your choice*
*I just hope and pray that your way of life*
*Bypasses your child's life*
*I pray that your child will be blessed with more knowledge*
*And wisdom than you ever had*
*I pray that your child will be blessed with happiness, success,*
*dignity, love*

*You on the other hand*
*Just hopeless and triflin*

81

*Tracy R. Offer*
*Copyright: 12/99*

*Tracy R. Offer*

# <u>*The Hardships of Love*</u>

*You meet a man, fall in love*
*If it works you get married, have children*
*You give him your all*
*Emotionally, physically, mentally*

*Suddenly, you become a no good bitch*

*You have worked just as hard as he has*
*You have sacrificed just as much as he has*
*In your heart you know this type of treatment isn't healthy*
*But because of the power of love, you stay*

*You have family, friends on the outside looking in*
*Telling you he isn't right for you*
*But once again, the power of love keeps you around*

*You begin to pray*
*Lord, please I know that there's another way*
*I am here today asking that you help me to help myself*
*Regain the strength, courage, and wisdom I once had*
*I am a better person, I deserve better*

*Suddenly, things began to change*
*All those harsh words, you cry no more*
*All those beatings, the pain you feel no more*

*Look at me now; I am stronger than before*
*I have regained my pride, my dignity*
*I hold my head up high, I stand tall, and proud*

*What goes around comes around*
*Do unto others, as you would have them do unto you*
*You reap what you sow*
*You call it revenge, but it's the way God made it*

*Look at you now*
*Jobless, lonely,*
*You have no one, your cry no one hears*

*Look at me*
*I have become successful in more ways than one*
*The power of love has taught me to be a better person to myself*

*Never give all you've got to give*
*In the end you will have nothing*

*Tracy R. Offer*
*Copyright: 07/99*
*All rights reserved*

*Tracy R. Offer*

# ***Do Unto Others***

When we first met I thought you were the sweetest person
*We talked on the phone for hours; I fell in love over the phone*

*You in turn showed you loved me too*
*At least I thought*

*We shopped, went places, just had good times*
*Things began to change*

*Every year on your anniversary*
*You would get cards, roses*
*There wasn't a holiday that came*
*That I didn't get you something*

*All because I loved you*

*No matter how much I showed you*
*I loved you*
*You accepted everything from me*
*And did what you felt like doing*

*You stayed out late nights*
*Females disrespected my home as well as me*
*You allowed your friends to interfere with out*
*Relationship; everything went down hill*

*In turn, you blamed me*
*Being a fool in love I accepted the blame*
*And continued to go out of my way to make*
*You happy*
*When all the time you were the blame*
*I blame myself for not seeing it sooner*

*Now, you say I am evil to you*
*Well, maybe the tables have turned for a reason*
*It's not being done purposely, it just happens*

*In the beginning it was me who treated you well*
*I was nothing but nice to you*
*I took all of your crap*

*At look at us now*
*You have done nothing to make things better*
*For us, the relationship, or the family*

*You ask, well what have I done*
*I did my share already*

*Tracy R. Offer*
*All Rights Reserved*
*Copyright: 12/99*

# <u>Death</u>

*You walk this earth, thinking it's yours*
*You do as you please and expect*
*Blessings to come your way*

*You treat others like crap, yet you want respect*
*You have yet to enter into my home,*
*Not once have you gotten on your knees*

*Day to day you are full of frustration*
*Wanting things to go so right, but you do wrong*

*You get on talk shows*
*Telling your business, acting like fools*

*You have done nothing to earn anything*
*But the trouble that comes your way*

*You plot the death of others,*
*You enjoy torturing those who are weaker than you*

*You can't defend yourself using your God given intelligence*
*Weapons and hatred are your only way out*

*You laugh as you kill*
*Well, are you prepared for your death?*

# ***Racist***

*What is the purpose?*

*We are all here struggling, no race is better than the next*

*We all have ancestors that were tortured for one reason or
another*

*No one should be taking from anyone
We can't base an entire race because of one bad apple*

*There's no race more powerful or more deserving than the next*

*We all have our own beliefs in life, but the one true belief is God*

*It isn't written that the world belongs to a particular race*

*However, it is written that
"Thou shall love thy enemy"*

*What pleasure does hatred give you?
Hate only reserves you a seat in Hell*

*You say you stand behind God and his word
Well, you must be far, far behind*

*There's only one God, and he surely does not approve of what
This world has become*

*I don't know what Bible you read,*
*I don't know where your teachings come from*
*But just a little advice, you may want to start changing your*
*ways*


*It may not seem like it, but our time here is short*
*And so is yours*


*Tracy R. Offer*
*All Rights reserved*
*Copyright: 12/99*

# <u>*No Fear*</u>

*Well, I have just read your letter*

*I would like to say that I agree with a few things*
*You are correct:*
*We can't hide, nor can we run*
*It's not because we can't; it's because we won't*

*The black generation is no longer afraid*
*We are here and won't be going anywhere until our God comes*

*We have done you no harm,*
*Years and years have passed us by*
*Still, you continue to think this world is yours*

*Well, we are all here temporarily and during that time nothing is*
*ours*

*You spend so much time trying to get back at us*
*Get back at us for what?*

*Our ancestors have struggled, and fought*
*Long and hard because we are humans just as you are*

*You call us niggas*
*Well, doesn't that mean stupidity?*
*What would you call yourselves?*

*No one put you in charge,*
*Your days are numbered just like everyone else's*

*We have no fear in our hearts,*
*There's nothing you can do to us that God can't fix*

*You have no idea what Judgement Day is, until God returns*

*To see the Mighty Prince Of Peace*
*Is the greatest thing for us*

*Just suppose he's black*
*How would you feel then?*

# ***<u>Stranger In My Mind</u>***

*During my daily routine; We meet again*
*So, we decided to exchange numbers*

*Wow, we had so much in common; our lives were so similar*

*We talked and talked as if we had known one another for years*

*Gradually, being with you seemed different*
*I started feeling uneasy in your presence*

*The thought of you no longer made me happy*
*Having you in my thoughts caused much discomfort*

*All the trust I put in you, all the secrets I shared*
*How could something such as this happen to me?*

*Reality check*
*I gave you not only my thoughts, dreams, fantasies*
*And trust, I gave you my life as well*

*You fixed my life for yourself*
*The secrets I shared, you shared also*
*You slept with my man, you showered my kids' with gifts*

*You didn't have a life of your own, so you tried to live mine*
*Well, thanks to your effort*
*You just made things stronger for my family and I*

*Still, you have no life*
*You were truly to good to be true*
*I am so full of anger for many reasons*
*I shared my everything with a stranger*
*Who I thought would be my best friend*
*Ha, you and the Devil should make amends*

*Never again, will I allow a stranger in my mind*

92



*Never again, will I allow a stranger in my mind*

# ***What Makes You A Man***

*You think because you have
Money, fancy cars, fine homes
You are a man?*

*You have brought many children into the world,
You show love to none of them, females shower you with gifts
and love
You are a man?*

*You don't even earn your money honestly,
And you say you are a man?*

*A man is someone who can wake up
Each and every morning thanking the Lord for seeing another
day*

*A man is not ashamed to take care of his children,
Nor does a man fear sensitivity*

*A man will have the strength and courage to get an honest job
Regardless of the pay, he will learn to take responsibility for his
actions*

*A man will not degrade a woman to make his self look good
Without us there would be no men*

*You can out drink and smoke your homies and you think you are
a beast
Your mother brought you into this world, did everything possible
to make sure
You had what you needed, she now needs you
Where are you?*

> *Take the time to take a real good look at yourself*
> *And ask "Am I a man?"*

94

# <u>***Society***</u>

*We put so much stress on ourselves as well as one another*

*Why do we worry about each other so much?*
*We have problems as individuals*

*We are so pressured about success*
*Looks, attire, education, personalities*
*If things don't go our way, we complain*

*It isn't up to us to change others*
*It's up to the individual to change*

*Who made us in charge?*
*Reality check, God is in charge*

*No matter who has more money*
*The biggest house, the fanciest vehicle*
*The prettiest children or who is more glamorous*

*When it comes to God, we are powerless little peons*

*No one is any better than the next person*
*We have gotten too caught up in the glamour of life,*
*We have forgotten how we are able to survive life*

*Money, power, respect, beauty, fashion*
*Has no meaning in Heaven, it's what's in the heart*

*We are destroying ourselves*
*Now we can't handle what we*
*Are bringing ourselves through*


*Society- a taste of Hell*


*Tracy R. Offer*
*Copyrights: 07/99*
*All rights reserved*

# **<u>Misery</u>**

*Why do we choose to live unhappy*
*Knowing it's unhealthy*

*Are we afraid of being alone?*

*They say misery loves company*
*What do you love misery or yourself?*

*Isn't the feeling of happiness more*
*Pleasurable than misery ?*

*Misery loves no one but itself,*
*You have to be strong within and know*
*What you want in life*

*Don't let a negative lifestyle control you*
*You are beautiful, wise, and strong*

*God made us as individuals with our own minds*
*Why let someone else tell you what to do?*

*You are you for a reason*
*You are special in your own way*
*Let no one else tell you differently*

*Only you know what's best for you*
*Let no one live your life for you*

*God is God for a reason*
*Talk to him*

*He can bring you peace of mind*
*Joy, happiness, and comfort*

*God can and will do all that you ask*
*As long as you keep your end of the deal*

*Look in the mirror*
*What do you see?*

*Don't let misery be the death of you*

*Tracy R. Offer*
*All Rights Reserved*
*Copyright: 07/99*

# ***Who is the Blame***

*Robbers-you can't keep or find a job*
*Molesters'/Rapist-you do what was done to you*
*Alcoholics/Drug Abusers-you feel there's no other way*

*You torture others' due to the things that may have*
*Happened to you during your childhood*

*Excuses, Excuses*
*Keep you from being punished*

*For years and years you have*
*Raped, robbed, abused, molested*

*You say it's because of the "white man"*
*You say it's because of your parents*
*You say it's because of the media*

*Well, you are the one that has done all those bad things*
*How can you blame someone else for your ignorance*

*You use mentally disturbed to escape reality*
*You sit on death row/life imprisonment*
*Saying how sorry you are and you want a second chance*

*Well, you need to be a man/woman*
*And face reality along with your responsibilities*

*There's no reason you should be put back on the streets*
*Children can no longer play in peace*
*Our elders can no longer sit in their homes in peace*

*You dare call yourself a man/woman*
*You prey on those that are not as strong as you*

*You may have escaped the justice system*
*But God sees your every move*

*So, when that day comes*
*God just may ask you "who is the blame"*

*What will your response be?*

# ***Why Cry Now***

*Throughout my childhood, I have made many*
*Mistakes, I have also learned from those mistakes*

*As I got older and took on adult responsibilities*
*I helped others from the heart*
*Took care of my grand and great grand children*

*Now I am old and lonely*
*No one bothers to call, write, or visit*

*You say I drive you crazy and all I do is brag about money*
*Well, I didn't have a grand life*
*So, I feel I have the right to brag about my accomplishments*

*After taking care of children, grandchildren, great grand's*
*You only know me when you need something,*
*Then have the nerve to get upset when I deny you the help*

*Well, the good Lord has given me a good life*
*Now my time has come*
*I lay here peacefully, surrounded by beautiful flowers*
*And the glorious sounds of hymns*

*As I lay here,*
*Think about the way you made me feel*
*The things you would say to me,*
*Times you shared with me, if any*

*Why do you cry now?*

*Tracy R. Offer*

*Copyright: 11/99*

## *About the Author*

Tracy R. Offer currently resides in the Montgomery County area working as an Accounts Payable Clerk for Execustay by Marriott.

She spent her years growing up in Seat Pleasant, MD (born in Baltimore, MD).

Poetry for Tracy is a way of relieving stress, and helping her to understand more about herself (i.e., where she has been, where she is going in life).

Tracy's poetry has hit home for many readers, touched many hearts and opened many minds.

I feel that I have become a stronger person, I have gone through many trials and tribulations in my life just like anyone else has, but the pain and misunderstandings of others about me and my purpose in life has stuck with me for quite some time.

It's time to let it all out; this is a benefit for me. I am able to write from my own life's experiences, listening, and feeling the pain of others; most of all I write from the heart.

There will be many that will or will not have any interests in my work; which is understandable. If we make an every day effort to please others, succeeding would be a grave challenge.

I have been told that I don't live by my poems. Well, my poetry has nothing to do with me. If someone gets to me, there's only so much I can take (just like anybody else) I am not going to let anyone try to control me or take advantage of me, I will definitely put you in your place-that's life, not my poetry.

Those who really know me, know and understand what my poems are about, those who have judged me and my poetry by only knowing me for a short period of time-Oh well, life goes on.

I am not here to live life for anyone else but me. I can't continue to let society's words put a hold on the things I want in life. My life is my own and yours is yours.

We spend so much time judging others whether a person is doing good or bad we still have something to say. I wonder what the world would be like if we took that same energy and tried to help feed the homeless families, helped the abused children, or even encouraged someone.

How much time would it take to say thank you? How much time would it take to say I love you?

I would like to thank God for allowing me to see a side of me that I didn't know existed; God has really been there for me throughout my life's experiences.

I would like to thank the African-American Website titled Timbook.tu for displaying my work, thank you to The International Library of Poetry, Poetry.com, The Society of Poets for acknowledging my work and given me my first break at publication. To all the readers who gave me their support and positive feedback, thank you and thanks to my family and friends who supported me as well. Also, I would like to thank the Directors' at The Score Learning Center, Potomac, MD.

Most of all, thanks to my daughters' who always keep me going and giving me something to write about.

Thank you all so much!